Let's Play!

by Kimberly Ring

Cover, ©Lori Adamski Peek/Stone/Getty Images; p.3, ©Harcourt; p.4, ©Dennis MacDonald/PhotoEdit; p.5, ©George Tiedemann/GT Images/Corbis; p.6, ©Joseph Sohm; Visions of America/CORBIS; p.7, ©Tami Chappell/Reuters/Corbis; p.8, ©AP Photo/Wade Payne; p.9, ©Jonathan Ferrey/Getty Images; p.10, ©Rachel Epstein/PhotoEdit; p.11, ©Duomo/CORBIS; p.12, ©Sarah Hadley/Alamy; p.13, ©Corbis/PunchStock; p.14, ©Ariel Skelley/CORBIS.

Printed in China

ISBN 10: 0-15-350007-7
ISBN 13: 978-0-15-350007-7

Ordering Options
ISBN 10: 0-15-349938-9 (Grade 3 ELL Collection)
ISBN 13: 978-0-15-349938-8 (Grade 3 ELL Collection)
ISBN 10: 0-15-357246-9 (package of 5)
ISBN 13: 978-0-15-357246-3 (package of 5)

1 2 3 4 5 6 7 8 9 10 985 12 11 10 09 08 07 06

There are many kinds of sports. You can have fun playing them. You can also cheer for your favorite team!

Soccer

Soccer is played on a field. There is a goal at each end. A goalkeeper guards the goal. Players try to kick the ball into the other team's goal. The team with the most goals wins.

Players can kick the ball. They can bounce the ball off their heads. Only goalkeepers can touch the ball with their hands!

Soccer players need to be good teammates. Good players share and pass the ball. They come to every practice.

The World Cup is played every four years. Teams from many countries play soccer with one another. One team wins the World Cup at the end. Winning makes a country proud.

Football

Football is a very popular sport in the United States. One team tries to move the football down the field. The team scores points by reaching the end of the field. The other team tries to keep the team from scoring. The other team tries to get the ball back.

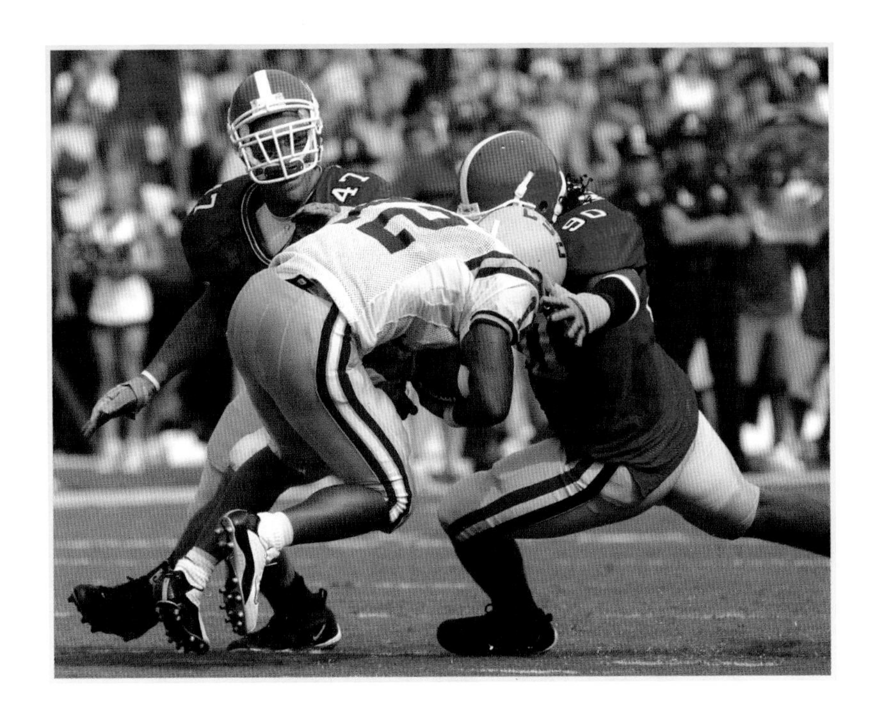

Football players work together as a team. The team has a coach. The players practice hard.

Football can be rough. Players push each other. The players wear pads and helmets so that they do not get hurt.

Basketball

The basketball player jumps. She slams the ball into the basket. The crowd cheers!

Basketball can be played indoors or outdoors. On each end of the court there is a hoop.

Players score by throwing the ball into the hoop. The players on the other team try to stop them. The other team tries to get the ball.

Baseball

Baseball is a game that many people love to play and to watch. The game is simple. Anyone can play.

One team is at bat. The other team's players stand in the field. They try to stop the batting team from scoring runs.

The pitcher throws the ball toward home plate. This throw is called a pitch. The batter tries to hit the ball with a bat. The ball can be difficult to hit because the pitcher throws it fast.

The batter can run to a base if the ball is hit. A player scores a run by going around all four bases.

If the batter swings at the ball but misses, it is a strike. When a batter gets three strikes, the batter is "out."

Hitting the ball out of the park is a home run. The batter can run around all the bases. A home run is one of the most exciting things in sports!

Baseball takes patience. It can be hard. It is also lots of fun.

There are many other sports. Some other sports are golf and tennis. Track and swimming are sports, too.

Sports are an exciting part of life. Playing a sport can keep you fit. Join in and have fun!

Scaffolded Language Development

Verb Tense Remind students that a verb tells the action in a sentence and that the tense of the verb tells the time of the action. Also remind students that some verbs have irregular past tenses. For example, the past tense of the verb *bring* is *brought.* Then read the sentences below. Help students to convert each sentence to past tense, and have them recite the new sentences chorally.

1. The catcher catches the ball.
2. The batter hits a homerun.
3. The quarterback runs with the ball.
4. The pitcher throws the ball.

Invite students to tell about a game they played recently. Encourage students to use the past tense in their responses. You may wish to model one example: *Yesterday, I played tag.*

Social Studies

States and Sports Ask students whether they know the names of any sports teams in your state and what sport each team plays. Make a list of students' responses. Then add to the list, if necessary. Finally, help students find the cities where the teams play on a map of your state.

School-Home Connection

Sports Talk Ask students to talk to friends or family members about sports. Have them find out which sports they like to play and why.

Word Count: 486